ENCOURAGE-MENT
—for—
PASTORS

compiled by JoNancy Sundberg

SHAW

ENCOURAGEMENT FOR PASTORS
A SHAW BOOK
PUBLISHED BY WATERBROOK PRESS
5446 North Academy Blvd., Suite 200
Colorado Springs, CO 80918
A division of Random House, Inc.

See acknowledgments at the end of the book.

ISBN 0-87788-205-3

Cover photo © 1998 by Image Technologies, Inc.
Typeset by Joyce Schram

Printed in Colombia.

04   03   02   01   00

10   9   8   7   6   5   4   3   2   1

CONTENTS

CONTENTS

INTRODUCTION

Father God,
Designer and Sustainer of all ministry,
please give . . .
>insight to fresh recruits,
>grit to the disheartened,
>anguish to the halfhearted,
>healing to the hurting,
>fervor to the lukewarm,
>energy to the fatigued,
>and vigor to the faithful. Amen.

H. B. London, Jr. and Neil Wiseman, Married to
a Pastor's Wife

✝

Oh, the utter extravagance of his work in
us who trust him.
Ephesians 1:19, THE MESSAGE

✝

We must run the race that lies ahead of us
and never give up.
Hebrews 12:1, GOD'S WORD

THE SUMMONS
God's Call

You did not choose me, but I chose you
and appointed you.

John 15:16, NIV

✝

The battle is the Lord's. He has called
you. He has honored you with a partner-
ship with Him. You are a unique and
extraordinary gift of grace God has given
to those you have been called to serve.
Don't ever forget it.

H. B. London, Jr. and Neil B. Wiseman, Pastors
at Risk

✝

Fear not, for I have redeemed you; I have
summoned you by name; you are mine. . . .
When you pass through the rivers, they
will not sweep over you. When you walk
through the fire, you will not be burned;
the flames will not set you ablaze. For I
am the LORD, your God, the Holy One of
Israel, your Savior.

Isaiah 43:1-3, NIV

May the LORD, the God of the spirits of all flesh, appoint a man over the congregation, who will go out and come in before them, and who will lead them out and bring them in, that the congregation of the LORD may not be like sheep which have no shepherd.

Numbers 27:16-17, NASB

Ultimately, our call to ministry rests upon our vision of God. A great God like this must be served. The greater our vision, the more compelling the call becomes. . . . The ministry is the highest of calls. We must never downplay or minimize it.

Kent and Barbara Hughes, Liberating Ministry from the Success Syndrome

He will be a vessel for honor, sanctified and useful for the Master, prepared for every good work.

2 Timothy 2:21, NKJV

The call of the Eternal must ring through the rooms of his soul as clearly as the sound of the morning-bell rings through the valleys of Switzerland, calling the peasants to early prayer and praise.

John Jowett, The Preacher: His Life and Work

The sovereign selection of God gives great confidence to Christian workers. We can truly say, "I am here neither by selection of an individual nor election of a group, but by the almighty appointment of God."

J. Oswald Sanders, Spiritual Leadership

I am Thine, O Lord, I have heard Thy
    voice,
And it told Thy love to me;
But I long to rise in the arms of faith,
And be closer drawn to Thee!

Consecrate me now to Thy service,
    Lord,
By the power of grace divine;
Let my soul look up with a steadfast
    hope,
And my will be lost in Thine.

Fanny J. Crosby, "I am Thine, O Lord"

But I have raised you up for this very purpose, that I might show you my power and that my name might be proclaimed in all the earth.

Exodus 9:16, NIV

We give thee but thine own,
What'er the gift may be;
All that we have is thine alone,
A trust, O Lord, from thee.
William W. How, "We Give Thee But Thine Own"

Then the LORD reached out, touched my
lips, and said to me, "Listen, I am giving
you the words you must speak."
Jeremiah 1:9, TEV

You go nowhere by accident. Wherever
you go, God is sending you. Wherever
you are, God has put you there. He has a
purpose in your being there. Christ who
indwells you has something He wants to
do through you wherever you are.
Richard C. Halverson

Were the whole realm of nature mine,
That were a present far too small.
Love so amazing, so divine,
Demands my soul, my life, my all!
*Isaac Watts, "When I Survey the Wondrous
Cross"*

Remember your calling!

GOAL POSTS
Personal Holiness

I urge you to live a life worthy of the calling you have received.
Ephesians 4:1, NIV

✝

In a word, we must labour for holiness of character. . . . You must have holiness: and, dear brethren, if you should fail in mental qualifications (as I hope you will not), and if you should have a slender measure of the oratorical faculty (as I trust you will not), yet, depend upon it, a holy life is, in itself, a wonderful power, and will make up for many deficiencies; it is, in fact, the best sermon the best man can deliver.

Charles H. Spurgeon, Lectures to My Students

✝

Create in me a clean heart, O God, and renew a steadfast spirit within me.
Psalm 51:10, NKJV

The highest priority God has for the pastor is that he put talking to God and establishing a close relationship with Him above every other priority—above ministry, above family, above his own desires.

E. Glenn Wagner and Glen S. Martin, Your Pastor's Heart

You will seek the LORD your God, and you will find Him if you seek Him with all your heart and with all your soul.

Deuteronomy 4:29, NKJV

I have one passion: it is He, He alone.

Count Nikolaus von Zinzendorf

God is not impressed with how much I know (intellectually) of His Word; He wants to know how much like Christ I am becoming.

Howard and William Hendricks, As Iron Sharpens Iron

He decided from the outset to shape the lives of those who love him along the same lines as the life of his Son.

Romans 8:29, THE MESSAGE

Intimacy with Christ nourishes ministry.
The pursuit of holiness keeps the soul in
shape.
Jerry Bridges

Holiness in us is the copy or transcript of
the holiness that is in Christ. As the wax
hath line for line the seal, and the child
feature for feature from the father, so is
holiness in us from Him.
Philip Henry

Take time to be holy;
Speak oft with thy Lord;
Abide in Him always,
And feed on His Word.

Take time to be holy;
The world rushes on;
Spend much time in secret
With Jesus alone.

By looking to Jesus,
Like Him thou shalt be;
Thy friends in thy conduct
His likeness shall see.
William D. Longstaff, "Take Time to Be Holy"

How little people know who think that holiness is dull. When one meets the real thing, it is irresistible!
C. S. Lewis

As the heart pants and longs for the water brooks, so I pant and long for you, O God. My inner self thirsts for God, for the living God.
Psalm 42:1-2, AMP

Let this be the greatest and final incentive to drink—that God is most glorified in us when we are the most satisfied in Him.
John Piper, The Pleasures of God

And let me not lay my pipe too short of
    the fountain,
  never touching the eternal spring,
  never drawing down water from
    above.
Puritan prayer, The Valley of Vision

The worth and excellency of a soul is to be measured by the object of its love.
Henry Scougal, The Life of God in the Soul of Man

Love the LORD your God with all your heart and with all your soul and with all your might.

Deuteronomy 6:5, NASB

Unless we know God deeply, we cannot love Him deeply.

R. C. Sproul, The Soul's Quest for God

And now just as you trusted Christ to save you, trust him, too, for each day's problems; live in vital union with him.... See that you go on growing in the Lord, and become strong and vigorous in the truth you were taught. Let your lives overflow with joy and thanksgiving for all he has done.

Colossians 2:6-7, TLB

The congregation is the pastor's place for developing vocational holiness. It goes without saying that it is the place of ministry . . . but it is also the place in which we develop virtue, learn to love, advance in hope—*become* what we preach. At the same time we proclaim a holy gospel, we develop a holy life. We dare not separate what we do from who we are.

Eugene H. Peterson, Under the Unpredictable Plant

God forbid that we should traffic in unlived truth.
H. A. Ironside

A message prepared in the mind reaches a mind; a message prepared in a life reaches a life.
Bill Gothard

But howsoever Thou dealest with me, only help me to continue to be perfectly satisfied with Thy holy will.
George Mueller, Autobiography of George Mueller

Prayer is surrender—surrender to the will of God and cooperation with that will. If I throw out a boathook from the boat and catch hold of the shore and pull, do I pull the shore to me, or do I pull myself to the shore? Prayer is not pulling God to my will, but the aligning of my will to the will of God.
E. Stanley Jones, A Song of Ascents

Prayer does not equip us for greater works—prayer is the greater work.
Oswald Chambers

Prayer ought to be frequent and fervent.
Martin Luther

Call to me and I will answer you and tell
you great and unsearchable things you
do not know.
Jeremiah 33:3, NIV

You can do more than pray after you
have prayed, but you cannot do more
than pray until you have prayed.
John Bunyan

Make my prayer as natural as breathing,
dear God. Give me an openness that will
welcome the fresh, the new. While I do
not seek novelty, I would at least like to
be sure that I have opened every possible
door to my soul.
Bernard Bangley, Near to the Heart of God

Speak to Him, thou, for He hears,
and Spirit with Spirit can meet—
Closer is He than breathing, and
nearer than hands and feet.
Alfred Lord Tennyson

It is possible to move men, through God
by prayer alone.
J. Hudson Taylor

Let us then approach the throne of grace
with confidence, so that we may receive
mercy and find grace to help us in our
time of need.

Hebrews 4:16, NIV

Remember your call!

The invitation to ministry is a call to become like Christ fully as much as it is to
do ministry. It keeps a pastor remember-
ing who he is and Whose he has become.

H. B. London, Jr. and Neil Wiseman, The Heart
of a Great Pastor

May God himself, the God of peace,
sanctify you through and through. May
your whole spirit, soul and body be kept
blameless at the coming of our Lord
Jesus Christ. The one who calls you is
faithful and he will do it.

1 Thessalonians 5:23-24, NIV

PEDESTALS
The Image Problem

Being "just a man" confuses and frustrates many pastors because the work of ministry demands so much more than mere human effort. Parishioners often refuse to accept the humanity of pastors. For whatever reason, nearly everyone wants their pastor to be bigger than life. But supermen do not exist in the church, only in the world of make-believe.

H. B. London, Jr. and Neil Wiseman, Married to a Pastor's Wife

✝

For we are God's workmanship, created in Christ Jesus to do good works, which God prepared in advance for us to do.

Ephesians 2:10, NIV

✝

This is the assigned moment for [Jesus] to move into the center, while I slip off to the sidelines.

John 3:30, THE MESSAGE

The most widely recognized ... barrier is the pedestal. Any of you can tell how it feels to be put on a pedestal. Most will admit that it is a bit dizzying up there, and that a fear of heights sets in. Some will confess that it is not all bad and in fact feels pretty good at times. ... I am sure all will agree that when you are deified it becomes increasingly difficult to say, "Wait a minute. I'm human."

Louis McBurney, Every Pastor Needs a Pastor

Foremost among the dangers is that he [the pastor] takes himself too seriously. Some preachers ... fall into this error. Spurgeon once characterized them as having their "neck-ties twisted around their souls."

Kent and Barbara Hughes, Liberating Ministry from the Success Syndrome

Much Christian leadership is exercised by people who do not know how to develop healthy, intimate relationships and have opted for power and control instead.

Henri Nouwen, In the Name of Jesus: Reflections on Christian Leadership

Power seduces pastors in every sized situation.
H. B. London, Jr. and Neil Wiseman, Pastors at Risk

Authority in itself never makes a leader unerring. . . . A pastor who insists on having his own way will . . . find himself followed by a group who submit to his domination but do not accept his leadership. He may hold a rope in his hand but it is not attached to anything that matters.
H. B. London, Jr. and Neil Wiseman, The Heart of a Great Pastor

My observation of Christendom is that most of us tend to base our personal relationship with God on our performance instead of His grace. If we've performed well, whatever well is in our opinion, then we expect God to bless us. If we haven't done well, our expectations are reduced accordingly. In that sense, we live by works rather than by grace. We are saved by grace. We are living by the sweat of our performance.
Jerry Bridges, Transforming Grace

For we do not preach ourselves but Christ Jesus as Lord, and ourselves as your bond-servants for Jesus' sake.
2 Corinthians 4:5, NASB

In the last part of the twentieth century, the church groans under the weight of a flawed assumption that its spiritual leaders must be well-educated, professional, and high-powered in order to be considered legitimate and worthy. The church as a whole pays a steep price for this false distinction, and these requirements create a dangerous pedestal from which leaders fall.
Stacy T. Rinehart, Upside Down: The Paradox of Servant Leadership

A reporter once asked the great evangelist D. L. Moody which people gave him the most trouble. He answered immediately, "I've had more trouble with D. L. Moody than any man alive."
John C. Maxwell, Developing the Leader Within You

We have met the enemy and he is us.
Pogo

Pride is the "in your face" attitude of the soul. . . . Self is the focus of pride. Pride seeks to defend and advance self in every way possible.

Joseph M. Stowell, Perilous Pursuits

All of you, clothe yourselves with humility toward one another, because, "God opposes the proud but gives grace to the humble." Humble yourselves, therefore, under God's mighty hand, that he may lift you up in due time.

1 Peter 5:5-6, NIV

We are like clay jars in which this treasure is stored. The real power comes from God and not from us.

2 Corinthians 4:7, CEV

Not that we are in any way confident of doing anything by our own resources— our ability comes from God.

2 Corinthians 3:5, PHILLIPS

The sufficiency of my merit is to know that my merit is not sufficient.

St. Augustine

When I survey the wondrous cross
On which the Prince of glory died,
My richest gain I count but loss,
And pour contempt on all my pride.

Forbid it, Lord, that I should boast
Save in the death of Christ, my God;
All the vain things that charm me most—
I sacrifice them to His blood.
Isaac Watts, "When I Survey the Wondrous Cross"

The choice is ours. Will we allow others to exalt us according to human standards? Or will we let God exalt us in His time and according to His standards? The answer is crucial. Leaders are susceptible to pride, yet God is opposed to the proud. We need to ask ourselves: Will I accept the praise of human beings or of God? If we do things for the praise of men, we already have our reward in full. Or do we believe God's Word to be true—that He will raise up the humble in due time?
Stacy T. Rinehart, Upside Down: The Paradox of Servant Leadership

Let another praise you, and not your own mouth—a stranger and not your own lips.
Proverbs 27:2, NRSV

When you enjoy praise you destroy it. If you delight in being praised you cease being worthy of it. It is impossible to praise the person who seeks praise. The one who is praised has done something worthwhile. The one who wants to be praised is merely arrogant.
Guigo I

Take care! Don't do your good deeds publicly, to be admired.
Matthew 6:1, NLT

If you act out of the pure love of God, you will not perform your actions to be seen by others. You will not even do them that *God* might notice them. If it were possible that your good works might escape God's attention, you would still perform them with the same joy, and in the same pureness of love.
John of the Cross, The Living Flame of Love

He has showed you, O man, what is good. And what does the LORD require of you? To act justly and to love mercy and to walk humbly with your God.
Micah 6:8, NIV

Remember your call!

God's sovereign searching of our hearts, and then His call to leadership, are awesome to behold. And they make a person very humble.

J. Oswald Sanders, Spiritual Leadership

The lowest station in the Lord's house is better than the highest position among the godless. To bear burdens and open doors for the Lord is more honor than to reign among the wicked. Every man has his choice, and this is ours. God's worst is better than the devil's best.

Charles H. Spurgeon

FISHBOWLS
Scrutiny and Isolation

The pastor is not only vulnerable because of involvement with his people, he is also vulnerable because he leads a public life. . . . The pastor and his family lead a fishbowl existence.

Kent and Barbara Hughes, Liberating Ministry from the Success Syndrome

✝

Pastors find it hard to open up and be vulnerable. They have carefully learned how to protect themselves; many live lonely lives, even in the midst of a lot of church activity.

Wes Roberts, Support Your Local Pastor

✝

Loneliness stalks where the buck stops.

Charles R. Swindoll, Man to Man

✝

Why do I have so many teachers and helpers and so few friends who are modest enough and wise enough simply to be companions with me in the becoming and the entering in?

Eugene H. Peterson, Under the Unpredictable Plant

A pastor, like any leader, often feels isolated. He seldom has a safe person with whom to share his loneliness, or feelings of failure, or doubts that God is caring for him.

Anonymous, Leadership

Too much privacy is unhealthy. Too many hours of independence easily leads to a fall—ethically or morally, financially or spiritually.

Charles R. Swindoll, Living Above the Level of Mediocrity

None of us was created to live in isolation. Life does not happen in a vacuum. We were created to live in relationship—with God, with ourselves, with others.

Wes Roberts, Support Your Local Pastor

It's lonely at the top, so you'd better take someone with you.
John C. Maxwell, The 21 Irrefutable Laws of Leadership

If one falls down, his friend can help him up. But pity the man who falls and has no one to help him up!
Ecclesiastes 4:10, NIV

Friendship is a sheltering tree.
Samuel Taylor Coleridge, "Youth and Age"

We belong to each other. We are the Lord's gifts to one another in the battles of life. We were never meant to fight alone without the Lord's help and the encouragement of one another.
Lloyd John Ogilvie, God's Best for My Life

Self-induced loneliness comes when we refuse to let anyone else into our heart and thoughts—the opposite of self-revelation. It is the all-too-common absurdity of refusing to be known, of keeping to our own thoughts, insisting on our privacy, and then wondering why nobody reaches out to us. As a result, laypersons think this withdrawal is a personal need for privacy, so they leave the minister and his family alone. This starts a vicious cycle that makes the pastor and his family even more lonely. You can clutch privacy so close to your chest that it closes your heart from welcoming those who love you the most.

H. B. London, Jr. and Neil Wiseman, Married to a Pastors Wife, *adapted*

There are no Lone Ranger leaders. Think about it: if you're alone, you're not *leading* anybody, are you?

John C. Maxwell, The 21 Irrefutable Laws of Leadership

We must be willing to receive from others as well as give to others. Some sacrificial souls delight in sacrificing themselves but are unwilling to allow others to reciprocate. They do not want to feel obligated to others. But leadership requires openness to others. To neglect receiving kindness and help is to isolate oneself, to rob others of opportunity, and to deprive oneself of sustenance.

J. Oswald Sanders, Spiritual Leadership

When we are lonely, we need an understanding friend. Jesus is the One who "sticks closer than a brother." When we

are lonely, we need strength to keep putting one foot in front of the other— Jesus is the One "who strengthens me."
Charles R. Swindoll, Growing Strong in the Seasons of Life

When you have shut the doors and made a darkness within, remember never to say that you are alone; for you are not alone, but God is within.
Epictetus

Yes, be bold and strong! Banish fear and doubt! For remember, the Lord your God is with you wherever you go.
Joshua 1:9, TLB

He who, from zone to zone,
Guides through the boundless sky thy
    certain flight,
In the long way that I must tread alone,
Will lead my steps aright.
William Cullen Bryant, "To a Waterfowl"

The solution is not to bury one's feelings in busyness or to run to an exotic resort. But living beyond loneliness is to be found in the positiveness of a task and the reality of one's Taskmaster. It is to be found in quietness in one's own backyard. It is not for sale, cannot be bartered for or negotiated. Yet, to live beyond loneliness is a state for which kings would exchange their fortunes.

Elizabeth Skoglund, Beyond Loneliness, *adapted*

Remember your call!

As the years roll on, the magnet of meaning which first attracts the pastor to ministry can be forgotten. . . . Return often to the vision given you when you started your present assignment. Polish the original vision. Preach it. Write about it. Be controlled by it. Celebrate the satisfaction ministry brings into your life. . . . Remember what God promised when He called you.

H. B. London, Jr. and Neil Wiseman, Pastors at Risk

GRASSHOPPERS
The Other Image Problem

We were like grasshoppers in our own sight.
Numbers 13:33, NKJV

✝

When we live by statistics, by comparing the odds, by numbering and measuring and weighing, the results are predictable: we become intimidated, crushed like grasshoppers by the giant heels of the challenges God has set before us.... And God gives us challenges, not to crush us, but to make us courageous.

Charles R. Swindoll, Living Above the Level of Mediocrity Study Guide

O God, our Father,
unless You help us,
we can see the idea,
but we cannot reach it;
we can know the right,
but we cannot do it;
we can recognize our duty,
but we cannot perform it;
we can see the truth,
but we can never wholly live by it.
O God, our Father, this day
we rest our weakness
in Your completeness.
Amen.

William Barclay, Prayers for the Christian Year

When God calls us, we cannot refuse
from a sense of inadequacy. Nobody is
worthy of such trust. When Moses tried
that excuse, God became angry. Let us
not pass the buck of leadership because
we think ourselves incapable.

J. Oswald Sanders, Spiritual Leadership

God's initial call to the ministry has very
little to do with ability or skill or exper-
tise. On the contrary, a call has
everything to do with faith, devotion and
yieldedness. A call starts most often at
the core of our being where God impacts

our identity and self-worth, and it moves outward to the needs of the world or to a hurting person next door or across town. A call tends to clarify the meaning of our life and to give us a purpose for living.

H. B. London, Jr. and Neil Wiseman, The Heart of a Great Pastor

I knew I had been called by God; I had never been able to escape that call, nor had I wanted to. But now I felt that I was the butt of a cruel joke. I was a failure. I wanted to quit. . . . One of the supreme glories of the gospel ministry is that our weakness is the opportunity for his power—our ordinariness for his extra-ordinariness.

Kent and Barbara Hughes, Liberating Ministry from the Success Syndrome

My power shows up best in weak people.

2 Corinthians 12:9, TLB

Consider what it means to have the Creator of all things know your name. Think of the comfort in knowing that the Great Physician has your best interests at heart. Ponder the security of knowing that the Good Shepherd is watching over you. Contemplate what it means that the Sav-

ior cared enough to die for you.... Jesus
loves you.

J. David Branon, Our Daily Bread

That you ... may be able to comprehend
with all the saints what is the width and
length and depth and height—to know
the love of Christ which passes knowledge.

Ephesians 3:17-19, NKJV

There is nothing you can do to make God
love you more! There is nothing you can
do to make God love you less! His love
is, unconditional, impartial, everlasting,
infinite, perfect. God is love.

Richard C. Halverson, Somehow Inside of Eter-
nity, *adapted*

Every man is intrinsically and infinitely
valuable by virtue of his creation in the
image of God, and that God esteems men
highly as evidenced by his sacrificial
death on the cross.

Louis McBurney, Every Pastor Needs a Pastor

Zushya, a Jewish rabbi who lived in the
Ukraine at the end of the eighteenth century, is remembered most for one
statement. He said, "In the world to

come, I will not be asked, 'Why weren't you Moses?' I will be asked, 'Why weren't you Zushya?'"

Larry Burkett and Rick Osborne, Your Child Wonderfully Made

We were given to one another by the Lord of the Body—because each one of us has a unique something to contribute—a piece of the divine puzzle no one else on earth can supply.

Charles R. Swindoll, Come Before Winter

Sometimes I struggle underground
just like a human mole and use self-pity
for a pick to dig a deeper hole.

There is no light upon my face, no place
to put my feet. My fearful heart begins to
race, I pat myself and weep.

Then I remember where I'm bound and
where I ought to be, I hurry up to higher
ground where Jesus walks with me.

Helene Stallcup, "Higher Ground"

The LORD will take delight in you.

Isaiah 62:4, NIV

Just think, you're here not by chance,
     but by God's choosing.
His hand formed you and made you the
     person you are.
He compares you to no one else—you
     are one of a kind.
You lack nothing that His grace can't
     give you.
He has allowed you to be here at this
     time in history
  to fulfill His special purpose for this
     generation.

Roy Lessin

Even when the leader has done the utmost to fulfill daily obligations, vast areas of work always remain. Every call for help is not necessarily a call from God, for it is impossible to respond to every need. If the leader sincerely plans his day in prayer, then executes the plan with all energy and eagerness, that is enough. A leader is responsible only for what lies within the range of control. The rest he should trust to our loving and competent heavenly Father.

J. Oswald Sanders, Spiritual Leadership

Now to him who is able to do immeasurably more than all we ask or imagine,

according to his power that is at work within us.
Ephesians 3:20, NIV

When Mother Teresa was asked how she could bear the truth that after many decades of ministering to those dying on the streets of Calcutta she had touched only one percent of them, she replied, "I was not called to be successful; I was only called to be faithful."
John A. Sanford, Ministry Burnout

Let us not get tired of doing what is right, for after a while we will reap a harvest of blessing if we don't get discouraged and give up.
Galatians 6:9, TLB

The Lord doesn't want our identity and self-worth as pastors to be bound up in results.
Steve R. Bierly, How to Thrive as a Small-Church Pastor

O Love of God, do this for me,
Maintain a constant victory.
Amy Carmichael, Edges of His Ways

But thanks be to God, who gives us the victory through our Lord Jesus Christ. Therefore, my beloved brethren, be steadfast, immovable, always abounding in the work of the Lord, knowing that your toil is not in vain in the Lord.
1 Corinthians 15:57-58, NASB

Entrust your efforts to the LORD, and your plans will succeed.
Proverbs 16:3, GOD'S WORD

You are responsible to do the best you can with what you've got for as long as you're able.
Charles R. Swindoll, Come Before Winter

Remember your call!
You did not choose me, but I chose you and appointed you to go and bear fruit—fruit that will last.
John 15:16, NIV

He clothes Himself with such as me,
Puts on my frail humanity.
Then using me to do His will
He can, in me, His work fulfill.
John Hunter, "Without Thee"

SIGNIFICANT OTHERS
Wife and Family

By wisdom a house is built, and through understanding it is established; through knowledge its rooms are filled with rare and beautiful treasures.

Proverbs 24:3-4, NIV

✝

Allow the quality of your family relationships to transform your home into a sanctuary where love, acceptance, affirmation, and accountability recharge your spiritual and emotional batteries. Use family togetherness to renew your whole being and to enrich each other. . . . Make your family the most significant people in your life.

H. B. London, Jr. and Neil Wiseman, Pastors at Risk

✝

He is the happiest, be he king or peasant, who finds peace in his home.

Goethe

If you are married, think back to your wedding and contrast those commitments against the ones you made at your ordination. In a basic sense, ordination covenants and marriage vows are in competition because both commitments are exclusive and binding; neither allows much room for the other.

H. B. London, Jr. and Neil Wiseman, Pastors at Risk

Resist marrying the church. That's adultery, because she is already married.

Louis McBurney, Leadership

Who can find a wife with a strong character? She is worth far more than jewels. Her husband trusts her with all his heart, and he does not lack anything good.

Proverbs 31:10-11, GOD'S WORD

Marriage brings together two people who are created in the image of God. They individually and as a couple reflect divine glory. Marriage is an awesome and wonderful union that has great potential for joy and celebration. . . . To love my wife truly and rightly, I must have a vision of how she is different from every other woman on the face of the earth. I must be captured by my wife's potential, her giftedness, her burdens, her passion.

Dan B. Allender and Tremper Longman III, Intimate Allies

You husbands likewise, live with your wives in an understanding way, as with a weaker vessel, since she is a woman; and grant her honor as a fellow heir of the grace of life, so that your prayers may not be hindered. To sum up, let all be harmonious, sympathetic, brotherly, kindhearted, and humble in spirit; not returning evil for evil, or insult for insult, but giving a blessing instead; for you were called for the very purpose that you might inherit a blessing.

1 Peter 3:7-9, NASB

Never condone public criticism of spouse or children—your promise of "until death do we part" was not to the church.

R. Michael and Rebecca Sanders, The Pastor's Unauthorized Instruction Book

Many pastors and their wives get together only in the car on the way to or from an activity. Once inside the church, they go to their separate areas of service. Rarely do they sit together or pray together. When the service is over, they circulate in different areas so they can touch as many people as possible. At last, the lights are out, the doors are closed, and they are off—to have company, be company, or go with others for ice cream and fellowship. By the time they get home, all their sparkle is gone, their personalities flat. They fall into bed, exhaustion overriding any chance for intimacy.

Anonymous, Leadership

Marriage is that relation between man and woman in which the independence is equal, the dependence is mutual, and the obligation reciprocal.

Louis K. Anspacher

Live together in harmony, live together in love, as though you had only one mind and one spirit between you. Never act from motives of rivalry or personal vanity, but in humility think more of each other than you do of yourselves.

Philippians 2:2-3, PHILLIPS

To keep your marriage brimming,
With love in he loving cup,
Whenever you're wrong, admit it,
Whenever you're right, shut up.
Ogden Nash

Even if marriages are made in heaven,
man has to be responsible for the mainte-
nance.
James C. Dobson

However you do it, the important thing is
to stay in contact and dialogue with
those the Lord has given to you for encouragement, understanding, challenge,
wisdom, prayer support, and love. This
includes someone right under your nose:
your spouse. My wife knows me better
than anyone else on the face of the earth.
She can, therefore, give me insight that
nobody else can give. Why would I want
to hurt myself and my ministry by cutting
myself off from my best counselor?
Steve R. Bierly, How to Thrive as a Small-
Church Pastor, *adapted*

It is in the home where our true success
or failure will be measured. The home is
the primary arena in which we must suc-

ceed if we are to be successful in any of
the others.
Steve Diggs, Free to Succeed

I used to tell my congregation at least
every six months, "I want you to know
that I love you. But you are a distant second compared to my family."
H. B. London, Jr., Refresh Renew Revive

To the church you are, sadly, expend-
able. To your family you are not.
R. Michael and Rebecca Sanders, The Pastor's
Unauthorized Instruction Book

Your family doesn't expect profound
perfection, command performances, or a
superhuman plan. Just you—warts and
all—your smile, your affirmation, your
gentleness, your support, your leadership, your involvement . . . *you!*
Charles R. Swindoll, Man to Man

We are to be all that Jesus Christ wants
them to be. They will then see us and imitate us, as we imitate God. . . . Our life is
to be lived for the Lord and for others—
in this case, our children.
Barb Snyder, Stand By Your Man

Children have more need of models than of critics.
French proverb

The greatest thing a father can do for his children is to love their mother.
Josh McDowell

What [kids] need is time—all they can get. Quantity time *is* quality time, whether you're discussing the meaning of the cosmos or just climbing on dad.
Jerry B. Jenkins, Loving Your Marriage Enough to Protect It

And you shall teach them diligently to your sons and shall talk of them when you sit in your house and when you walk by the way and when you lie down and when you rise up.
Deuteronomy 6:7, NASB

Remember your call!
He must be one who manages his own household well, keeping his children under control with all dignity (but if a man does not know how to manage his own household, how will he take care of the church of God?).
1 Timothy 3:4-5, NASB

Effective pastors for the new century
must be whole persons who deliberately
balance being and doing, family and
church, person and profession, worship
and work.

H. B. London, Jr. and Neil Wiseman, Pastors at
Risk

RUBBER BANDS
Stress and Priorities

I once heard stress in life equated to a rubber band. If you string a rubber band around a stack of papers and leave it there, stretched to the max for a long, long time, when you attempt to remove the band from that pile of papers, often the rubber band breaks. We've all had that happen. But if you take a rubber band of fair quality and stretch it, then relax it, then stretch it, then relax it, then stretch it, then relax it, you can do that for a long time without the rubber band breaking.

Wes Roberts, Support Your Local Pastor

✝

I sat at my desk and looked at the two books. One was my Bible, the other my Day-Timer. They were at war again. Personal devotions versus professional duties.

Richard Bridston, Leadership

There has never been a more stress-ridden society than ours. . . . Stress has become a way of life; it is the rule rather than the exception. . . . Those who soar above mediocrity are people with priorities. They think in terms of who and what are first in the home, at work, in possessions, and in relationships as well. People who have priorities keep that in perspective.

Charles R. Swindoll, Stress Factors, Living Above the Level of Mediocrity

With people and projects pulling him from all directions, the pastor must be very wise in how he schedules his day. If he is not careful, the good things may squeeze out the important, even crucial things. He needs to have the mind of the Lord for each day and be willing to let the Lord interrupt where necessary. He needs discernment to know when an interruption is from the Lord and when it is from another source.

E. Glenn Wagner and Glen S. Martin, Your Pastor's Heart

If you're conscientious in ministry, you never get a day's work done. You always

see more needs at the end of a day than you recognized at the beginning.
Ben Haden

If we string ourselves out, expending 100 percent of our time and energy, there is no way in which we can adjust to the unexpected emergency. We become defensive about our expended energies because there isn't anything left to give.
Louis H. Evans, Jr., Covenant to Care

What are we called to do? . . . What are the necessities without which we cannot get along? Everything else has to be considered negotiable: discretionary, not necessary.
Gordon MacDonald, Ordering Your Private World

There is only so much sand in the hourglass. Who gets it?
Max Lucado, In the Eye of the Storm

Make the best use of your time.
Ephesians 5:16, PHILLIPS

If you're Noah, and your ark is about to sink, look for the elephants first, because you can throw over a bunch of small animals and your ark will keep sinking. But

if you can find one elephant to get over-
board, you're in much better shape.

Vilfredo Pareto, adapted

Efficiency is doing things right and ef-
fectiveness is doing right things.

Peter Drucker

Activity is not necessarily accomplish-
ment.

John C. Maxwell, The 21 Irrefutable Laws of
Leadership

How can I persuade a person to live by
faith and not by works if I have to juggle
my schedule constantly to make everything fit into place?

Eugene H. Peterson, The Contemplative Pastor

Before all things, even service to God,
we must love God with all of our hearts.
It is the highest priority in life. . . . In the
cold, hard business world there are few
things more important to success than
learning how to set priorities and live by
them. It is no less important in the spiritual life . . . and in the spiritual realm the
number one priority is loving God.

Kent and Barbara Hughes, Liberating Ministry
from the Success Syndrome

Each of us has the time to do the whole will of God for our lives.
J. Oswald Sanders, Spiritual Leadership

I can do all things through Christ which strengtheneth me.
Philippians 4:13, KJV

The never-done dimension of ministry holds the potential for discouragement, but seen another way it provides a rewarding challenge. Writes Deane Kemper, "The most satisfying activities in life are those we can never completely master." The fact ministry is never completed says something about its greatness.
Kevin A. Miller, Leadership

But the Lord stood at my side and gave me strength, so that through me the message might be fully proclaimed and all the Gentiles might hear it.
2 Timothy 4:17, NIV

There is another side of stress that is easily overlooked, and that is trying to do too much ourselves. All of us have a limit.
Charles R. Swindoll, Stress Fractures

The thing that you are doing is not good. You will surely wear out, both yourself and these people who are with you, for the task is too heavy for you; you cannot do it alone.

Exodus 18:17-18, NASB

In [the] Word, we clearly see that team ministry is supposed to be the rule, not the exception. Aaron and Hur held Moses' hands up when he grew tired. Jonathan helped David find strength in the Lord. Jesus sent out His followers two by two. Paul traveled with missionary companions.

Steve R. Bierly, How to Thrive as a Small-Church Pastor

But find some capable, honest men who fear God. . . . They will help you carry the load, making the task easier for you.

Exodus 18:21-22, NLT

Know your limitations—refer, refer, refer.

R. Michael and Rebecca Sanders, The Pastor's Unauthorized Instruction Book

I thought
   I needed **IT**.
Why, I could even
   use **IT** for Him!
Then, I found out
   IT had needs—
Polishing, upgrading,
   assembling, restoring
And **I** was the
   one being used.
JoNancy Sundberg

He who buys what he doesn't need steals
from himself.
Swedish proverb

Think about these false gods [a thing, a
person, riches] as weeds in your garden.
Pull them out by the root. Set your heart
on nothing that is not God. Love God
with your whole heart. Do everything for
his sake.
Thomas Cranmer, Catechismus

Whatever is in first place, if it isn't Christ
alone, it is in the wrong place.
Charles R. Swindoll, Living Above the Level of
Mediocrity

Strangely, the one thing we need is the last thing we consider. We've been programmed to think that fatigue is next to godliness. That the more exhausted we are (and look!), the more spiritual we are and the more we earn God's smile of approval.

Charles R. Swindoll, Man to Man

Come to me, all you who are weary and burdened, and I will give you rest. Take my yoke upon you and learn from me, for I am gentle and humble in heart, and you will find rest for your souls.

Matthew 11:28-29, NIV

You chart the path ahead of me, and tell me where to stop and rest.

Psalm 139:3, TLB

Margin is the space between our load and our limits. . . . Actually, margin is not a spiritual necessity. But availability is. God expects us to be available for the needs of others. And without margin, each of us would have a great difficulty guaranteeing availability. Instead, when God calls, He gets the busy signal.

Richard A. Swenson, The Overload Syndrome, Margin

Six days do your work, but on the seventh day do not work, so that [all] may be refreshed.

Exodus 23:12, NIV

Sabbath: Uncluttered time and space to distance ourselves from the frenzy of our own activities so we can see what God has been and is doing. . . . So few pastors keep a Sabbath. . . . How can we quit work for a day when we have been commanded to redeem the time? How can we shut up when we have fire in our mouth? How can we do nothing for a whole day when we have been told on high authority to be urgent in season and out of season, and there is never a season in which the calls for help do not exceed our capacity to meet them?

Eugene H. Peterson, Working the Angles

Seasons of solitude with God enable us to see life and ministry accurately.

H. B. London, Jr. and Neil Wiseman, Pastors at Risk

Solitude is the one place where we can gain freedom from the forces of society that will otherwise relentlessly mold us.

John Ortberg, The Life You've Always Wanted

But those who hope in the LORD will renew their strength. They will soar on wings like eagles; they will run and not grow weary, they will walk and not be faint.

Isaiah 40:31, NIV

Remember your call!

I fear failure, and therefore am tempted to sacrifice integrity on the altar of success. I fear unemployment, and am tempted to compromise the Word to keep my position as preacher of that Word. Sloth sneaks under the door of my study and whispers, "Relax, no one will know the difference between an aorist and a perfect tense—don't waste your time." I have allowed my schedule to become overcrowded and have forfeited much-needed study time. A host of other lame excuses could be offered, none of which would stand the righteous scrutiny of Him who has called me to the pulpit—His pulpit, where His Word is to be preached. The pulpit is no place for the coward.

Robert Hopper, Tabletalk Magazine

In those times when we stumble for our footing in the awful swellings of the Jordan, and the Evil One whispers in our ear, "Why did you ever decide to be a preacher anyway?" the right answer can only be, "Cause I was called, you fool!"

Timothy George, Christianity Today

Serpents
Temptation and Accountability

Temptations come packaged in varied shapes, sizes, and colors . . . but most of them fall into one of three categories:

1. Material Temptation—This is lust for things.
2. Personal Temptation—This is lust for status.
3. Sensual Temptation—This is lust for another person.

We tend to forget when we're tempted: God is there through it all. He is faithful. We may feel alone, but we are not alone. He places definite limitations on the attack.

Charles R. Swindoll, Man to Man, Stress Fractures

✝

You are tempted in the same way that everyone else is tempted. But God can be trusted not to let you be tempted too much, and he will show you how to escape from your temptations.

1 Corinthians 10:13, CEV

Do you know what lies right between you and your next sin? Something called a "temptation." Therefore, the moment you become serious about "personal holiness" is the moment you must also become serious about "times of temptation." . . . .Temptations are the entry door to every sin.
Bruce H. Wilkinson, Victory Over Temptation

Cling to discipline.
Do not relax your grip on it.
Keep it because it is your life.
Do not stray onto the path of wicked
    people.
Do not walk in the way of evil people.
Avoid it.
Do not walk near it.
Turn away from it,
and keep on walking.
Proverbs 4:13-15, GOD'S WORD

Temptation is not only an opportunity to do the wrong thing, it is also an opportunity to do right.
Stuart Briscoe

You fall the way you lean.
Anonymous

Temptations discover what we are.
Thomas a Kempis

Spiders are not deadly to bees, but they entangle their honeycombs with webs and make their work difficult. Tiny sins will not kill your soul, but if they wrap a tangle of bad habits around you, devotion will suffer. . . . The evil is not in the pastimes; it is in our affection for them. Don't sow weeds in the soil of your heart. Your garden space is limited.
Francis de Sales, The Devout Life

The chains of habit are too weak to be felt until they are too strong to be broken.
Samuel Johnson

Daniel Webster was asked, "What is the greatest thought that can occupy a man's mind?" He said, "His accountability to God."
Abel Ahlquist

For a man's ways are in full view of the LORD, and he examines all his paths.
Proverbs 5:21, NIV

Any great leader who has integrity has someone to hold him in account, be that

"someone" a group of people, one man, or a covenant-relationship partner. But there must be someone who's not afraid to ask the tough questions.
John C. Maxwell

Give instruction to a wise man, and he will be yet wiser: teach a just man, and he will increase in learning.
Proverbs 9:9, KJV

Lord, I am willing
To receive what You give
To lack what You withhold
To relinquish what You take
To suffer what You inflict
To be what You require.
And, Lord, if others are to be
Your messengers to me,
I am willing to hear and heed
What they have to say. Amen
Accountability has a way of keeping one's private life squeaky clean.
Charles R. Swindoll, Living Above the Level of Mediocrity

People who want to get rich fall into temptation and a trap and into many foolish and harmful desires that plunge men into ruin and destruction. For the love of money is a root of all kinds of evil. Some people, eager for money, have wandered from the faith and pierced themselves with many griefs.

1 Timothy 6:9-10, NIV

The demon in money is greed. Nothing can destroy human beings like the passion to possess. . . . The demon in sex is lust. Lust captivates rather than emancipates. . . . Power destroys relationships. Power's ability to destroy human relationships is written across the face of humanity.

Richard Foster, Money, Sex and Power

Help me, Lord to be alert to authenticity. Let me neither manipulate or be manipulated. Above all, keep me honest in my life of faith.

Bernard Bangley, Near to the Heart of God

Resolved, Never to do any thing which I should be afraid to do if it were the last hour of my life.

Jonathan Edwards, The Works of Jonathan Edwards

So, if you think you are standing firm, be careful that you don't fall!
1 Corinthians 10:12, NIV

The real battlefield for the Christian is the mind. . . . No secrets are kept from God. . . . The goal of our secret thought life, since it is no secret from God, should be to live a life of personal holiness.
Patrick Morley

What we think about when we are free to think about what we will—that is what we are or will soon become.
A. W. Tozer, Born After Midnight

Take captive every thought to make it obedient to Christ.
2 Corinthians 10:5, NIV

If you don't make up your mind, your unmade mind will unmake you.
E. Stanley Jones

Good thoughts bear good fruit, bad thoughts bear bad fruit—and man is his own gardener.
James Allen

Guard the doorway of your heart. Submit your thoughts to the authority of Christ. The more selective you are about seeds, the more delighted you will be with the crop.

Max Lucado, Just Like Jesus

May the mind of Christ, my Savior,
Live in me from day to day,
By His love and pow'r controlling
All I do and say.

Kate B. Wilkinson, "May the Mind of Christ, My Savior"

It is God's will that you should be sanctified: that you should avoid sexual immorality; that each of you should learn to control his own body in a way that is holy and honorable, not in passionate lust like the heathen.

1 Thessalonians 4:3-5, NIV

It is with our passions as it is with fire and water. They are good servants but bad masters.

Sir Roger L'Estrange

Self-indulgence has slain its thousands; let us tremble lest we perish by the hands of that Delilah. Let us have every passion and habit under due restraint: if we are not masters of ourselves we are not fit to be leaders in the church.

Charles H. Spurgeon, Lectures to My Students

You may be surprised to know that every time the subject of sensual lust is discussed in the New Testament, there is one invariable command—*run!* We are told to get out, to flee, to run for our lives. It is impossible to yield to temptation while running in the opposite direction.

Charles R. Swindoll, Man to Man

Flee [separate yourself] from youthful lusts, and *pursue* [separate yourself to] righteousness, faith, love and peace, with those who call on the Lord from a pure heart.

2 Timothy 2:22, NASB (italics and brackets, Bruce H. Wilkinson, Personal Holiness in Times of Temptation)

Human beings have a remarkable capacity for self-deception.

John Ortberg, The Life You've Always Wanted

O what a tangled web we weave,
When first we practice to deceive!

Sir Walter Scott

The life which is unexamined is not worth living.
Plato

For accountability to work, you must cultivate the skill of listening to the advice of others. This is not a time for the red flag of reaction, but for the white flag of surrender.
Charles R. Swindoll, Living Above the Level of Mediocrity Study Guide

Iron sharpens iron, so one man sharpens another.
Proverbs 27:17, NASB

When a preacher of righteousness has stood in the way of sinners, he should never again open his lips in the great congregation until his repentance is as notorious as his sin.
John Angell James

Remember your call!
For all those who have received a call to ministry, . . . it is primarily a call to holiness, and a call which brings with it high spiritual expectations.
Kent and Barbara Hughes, Liberating Ministry from the Success Syndrome

Certainly, the task facing [the] pastor is great and the standard he must meet is high. But then again, so is his calling. He is rightly held to that standard and he is rightly disqualified if he falls short.

John MacArthur, Jr.

GOLIATHS
Expectations and Finances

The Lord said, "Lay not up for your-selves treasures on earth," and the church has rallied to the command in behalf of their minister! It is a good thing Paul said "a workman is worthy of his hire," or we'd probably pay nothing at all.

Louis McBurney, Every Pastor Needs a Pastor

✝

The ministering person is dealing con-stantly with people's expectations. He can wear himself out trying to satisfy [them], or exhaust himself in anxiety be-cause he cannot.

John A. Sanford, Ministry Burnout

✝

Turn your Goliath over to Jehovah, the giant-killer. Explain to your powerful God how anxious you are for Him to win this victory for a change—not the giant, and not you.

Charles R. Swindoll, Come Before Winter

We all live with the tension between what we are and what others want us to be. We'd like to fulfill the exalted expectations that many people have for us, but we can't.

Erwin Lutzer, Pastor to Pastor

Everyone continually deals with a two-way interplay of expectations; (1) what others expect of them and (2) what they expect of others. No one can totally avoid or abolish the impact expectations have on the details of living.

H. B. London, Jr. and Neil Wiseman, Married to a Pastor's Wife

When we put too many expectations on others, they return the favor. In this hyper-critical, grace-devoid, expectation-overloaded world, we need to set one another free. When we expect too much of others, we suffocate them. . . . We frustrate ourselves.

Richard A. Swenson, The Overload Syndrome

Some time ago, from both sides of the pulpit, we created a monster when we laid out the expectations, verbal and non-verbal, that pastors cannot have

"downside" emotions. That's depressing. Life is not all "up," not all bright days with warm, balmy breezes. Some days are the "pits" in ministry, and in life.
Wes Roberts, Support Your Local Pastor

Be careful of buying into the myths of what a pastor should have as innate gifts and abilities, of what he should or should not do. Most pastors bear weighty expectations as leaders. Those weights tend to weaken both your pastor's dedication to his calling and his ability to get it done.
E. Glenn Wagner and Glen S. Martin, Your Pastor's Heart

The qualifications of a pastor:
1. The mind of a scholar
2. The heart of a child.
3. The hide of a rhinoceros.
Stuart Briscoe

Expecting too little of ourselves is wasteful; expecting too much of ourselves is folly.
William A. Ward

Many expectations are homemade and come from our own inner world. Often we are the only one in the congregation who holds them. But as long as expectations control us, our feelings of helplessness, powerlessness, and servitude will increase.... Expectations are a part of life we cannot avoid. Nor should we try. It is more useful to find ways to transform, confront, change, use, and even embrace them. Then we may even learn to welcome the reasonable expectations of others.

H. B. London, Jr. and Neil Wiseman, Married to a Pastor's Wife

Often the pressure a spiritual leader feels comes from assuming tasks that God has not assigned; for such tasks the leader cannot expect God to supply the extra strength required.

J. Oswald Sanders, Spiritual Leadership

Am I a prisoner of people's expectations or liberated by divine promises?
Henri Nouwen

1. You will seldom get what you deserve from people, so don't expect it.
2. You will always get what is best from God, so don't doubt it.

3. Your ability to handle both is directly related to the consistency of your walk with the Lord.

Charles R. Swindoll, Man to Man

All ministry expectations that truly matter are rooted and nourished by prayer and Scripture. How freeing it is to be assured that the Father's expectations of us are reasonable, doable, and productive. He expects our best, and He knows exactly what that is.

H. B. London, Jr. and Neil Wiseman, Married to a Pastor's Wife

This should be our prayer and our goal, that when the last day comes, when we stand before the tribunal of God, Christ will take delight in what He sees and bless us.

Tabletalk Magazine, *Ligonier Ministries*

Our personal attitude toward a modest salary always improves when we remember for whom we ultimately work. God's praise is a mighty high payoff, much more desirable than money.

H. B. London, Jr. and Neil Wiseman, Pastors at Risk

I have been young and now I am old. And in all my years I have never seen the Lord forsake a man who loves him; nor have I seen the children of the godly go hungry.

Psalm 37:25, TLB

Look, if God called you to that particular assignment in that particular location, then He is the one who is also providing the income for you.

Ron Blue

"Test me in this," says the LORD Almighty, "and see if I will not throw open the floodgates of heaven and pour out so much blessing that you will not have room enough for it."

Malachi 3:10, NIV

The king of love my Shepherd is,
Whose goodness faileth never;
I nothing lack if I am His
and He is mine forever.

And so thro' all the length of days
Thy goodness faileth never;
Good Shepherd, may I sing Thy praise
within Thy house forever.

Henry W. Baker, "The King of Love My Shepherd Is"

Remarkable. Sometimes God is so touched by what He sees that He gives us what we need and not simply that for which we ask.
Max Lucado, The Gift for All People

The soul is measured by its flights,
Some low and others high,
The heart is known by its delights,
And pleasures never lie.
John Piper, The Pleasures of God

It is a mistake to love things that will inevitably decay, and to be annoyed when they do.
Guigo I, Meditations

Measure wealth not by the things you have, but by the things you have that you would not take money for.
Russ Crosson

For I have learned, in whatsoever state I am, therewith to be content.
Philippians 4:11, KJV

Contentment lies not in what is yours, but in whose you are.
Doug Trouten, Twin Cities Christian

The LORD will guide you continually, and satisfy your needs . . . and you shall be like a watered garden, like a spring of water, whose waters never fail.

Isaiah 58:11, NRSV

Remember your call!

Ministry is tomfoolery without a sacred summons.

H. B. London, Jr. and Neil Wiseman, The Heart of a Great Pastor

And we know that God causes all things to work together for good to those who love God, to those who are called according to His purpose.

Romans 8:28, NASB

DRAGONS
Problem Encounters

Dragons, of course, are fictional beasts. They exist only in the imagination. But there are dragons of a different sort, decidedly real. They are often sincere, well-meaning saints, but they leave ulcers, strained relationships, and hard feelings in their wake. Dragons are best known for what comes out of their mouths. At times their mouths are flame throwers; other times the heat and smoke are not apparent, but the noxious gas does the damage. Their tongues may be smooth, but they are forked. . . . They also wreak destruction.

Marshall Shelley, Well-Intentioned Dragons

✝

As we go through the deep waters of ministry, remember that their purpose is not to drown us but to cleanse us.

H. B. London, Jr., Refresh Renew Revive

If what they are saying about you is true, mend your ways. If it isn't true, forget it, and go and serve the Lord.
Harry A. Ironside

Don't refuse to accept criticism; get all the help you can.
Proverbs 23:12, TLB

Even dragons can sometimes be right, and almost all pastors are willing to benefit if the criticism is valid.
Marshall Shelley, Well-Intentioned Dragons

The trouble with most of us is that we'd rather be ruined by praise than loved by criticism.
Norman Vincent Peale

Problems are God's chisel to shape the soul. He tests us to develop us, and He urges us not to give up or perform an abortion on His divine purposes. Testing sculpts us to more closely resemble Jesus Christ. We all want the product of Christlikeness, but we shun the process.
Howard G. Hendricks, Color Outside the Lines

God whispers to us in our pleasures, speaks to us in our conscience, but shouts in our pains; it is His megaphone to rouse a deaf world.

C. S. Lewis, The Problem of Pain

When through fiery trials
thy pathway shall lie,
My grace, all sufficient,
shall be thy supply:
The flame shall not hurt thee;
I only design
Thy dross to consume,
and thy gold to refine.

Rippon's Selection of Hymns, "How Firm a Foundation"

It's doubtful that God can use any man greatly until he's hurt deeply.

A. W. Tozer

If an enemy were insulting me, I could endure it; if a foe were raising himself against me, I could hide from him. But it is you, a man like myself, my companion, my close friend, with whom I once enjoyed sweet fellowship as we walked with the throng at the house of God.

Psalm 55:12-14, NIV

For wolves to worry lambs is no wonder, but for lambs to worry one another, this is unnatural and monstrous.

Thomas Brookes

If it is possible, as much as depends on you, live peaceably with all men.

Romans 12:18, NKJV

Conflict is common and not necessarily bad. Conflict happens because we are all different. And we are all different because God, in His infinite wisdom, chose to make each one of us different.

Gary J. Oliver, Real Men Have Feelings Too

To have conflict is human, to have grace is divine. In our fallen nature, we will experience pain in relationships. Usually, at least in part, it will be of our making. As we respond with grace, we allow God to work further in us. He is glorified. The church is edified. And the world again witnesses that in all our differences, we truly love one another.

H. B. London, Jr., Refresh Renew Revive

Resolved: that all men should live for the glory of God. Resolved second: that whether others do or not, I will.
Jonathan Edwards

Do not repay evil with evil or insult with insult, but with blessing, because to this you were called so that you may inherit a blessing.
1 Peter 3:9, NIV

Don't get involved in foolish, ignorant arguments that only start fights. The Lord's servants must not quarrel but must be kind to everyone. They must be able to teach effectively and be patient with difficult people.
2 Timothy 2:23-24, NLT

It is difficult not only to say the right thing in the right place, but far more difficult to leave unsaid the wrong thing at the tempting moment.
George Sala

Bear with each other and forgive whatever grievances you may have against one another. Forgive as the Lord forgave you.
Colossians 3:13, NIV

You must live with the people to know their problems and live with God in order to solve them.

P. T. Forsyth

One of the best ways to lead people into a willing spirit is to model it. That involves things like reaching out without being invited and sensing deep hurts without being told. . . . It is impossible to give of ourselves at arm's length. Personal involvement is essential, not incidental.

Charles R. Swindoll, The Gentle Art of a Servant's Heart

May God who gives patience, steadiness, and encouragement help you to live in complete harmony with each other—each with the attitude of Christ toward the other. And then all of us can praise the Lord together with one voice, giving glory to God, the Father of our Lord Jesus Christ.

Romans 15:5-6, TLB

Clothe yourselves with compassion, kindness, humility, gentleness and patience.

Colossians 3:12, NIV

Christ said that our relationships with each other are so significant and so central to the gospel that He gave the world the right to judge the validity of His message by the love they observed among us: "By this all men will know that you are My disciples, if you have love for one another" (John 13:35, NASB).

Stacy T. Rhinehart, Upside Down: The Paradox of Servant Leadership

To love at all is to be vulnerable. Love anything, and your heart will certainly be wrung and possibly broken. If you want to make sure of keeping it intact, you must give your heart to no one.

C. S. Lewis, The Four Loves

Love knows no limit to its endurance, no end to its trust, no fading of its hope; it can outlast anything. Love never fails.

1 Corinthians 13:7-8, PHILLIPS

I praise You for Your sovereignty over the broad events of my life and over the details. With You, nothing is accidental, nothing is incidental, and no experience is wasted. You hold in Your own power my breath of life and all my destiny. And every trial that You allow to happen is a

platform on which You reveal Yourself,
showing Your love and power, both to
me and to others looking on.
Ruth Myers, 31 Days of Praise

Remember your call!

We must realize there's a cost to our calling. The Man we're following said to us,
"Come after Me, take up your cross, and
follow Me." To sense that we and our
work are rejected is not fun. But our Savior was "despised and rejected of
men." . . . We ought not to be so surprised.
Suffering, sacrifice, and submission are
what ministry is about. Ask Paul.
H. B. London, Jr., Refresh Renew Revive

Only fear the LORD and serve Him in
truth with all your heart; for consider
what great things He has done for you.
1 Samuel 12:24, NASB

We are going to ordain you to this ministry and we want your vow that you will
stick with it. This is not a temporary assignment but a way of life that we need
lived out in our community. . . . Your task
is to keep telling the basic story, repre-
senting the presence of the Spirit,
insisting on the priority of God, speaking

the biblical words of command and promise and invitation.

Eugene H. Peterson, Working the Angles

CONCLUSION

We've been surrounded and battered by troubles, but we're not demoralized; we're not sure what to do, but we know that God knows what to do; we've been spiritually terrorized, but God hasn't left our side; we've been thrown down, but we haven't broken. What they did to Jesus, they do to us. . . . While we're going through the worst, you're getting in on the best!

2 Corinthians 4:8-12, THE MESSAGE

Therefore, since through God's mercy we have this ministry, we do not lose heart.

2 Corinthians 4:1, NIV

Did we in our own strength confide,
Our striving would be losing,
Were not the right man on our side,
The man of God's own choosing.
Dost ask who that may be?
Christ Jesus, it is He—
Lord Sabaoth His name,
From age to age the same,

And He must win the battle.
Martin Luther, "A Mighty Fortress Is Our God"

In Christ we have a love that can never be fathomed, a life that can never die, a peace that can never be understood, a rest that can never be disturbed, a joy that can never be diminished, a hope that can never be disappointed, a glory that can never be clouded, a light that can never be darkened, and a spiritual resource that can never be exhausted.
Author unknown, Our Daily Bread

What does the LORD your God ask of you but to fear the LORD your God, to walk in all his ways, to love him, to serve the LORD your God with all your heart and with all your soul, and to observe the LORD's commands and decrees that I am giving you today for your own good?
Deuteronomy 10:12-13, NIV

Lord of ministry,
Protect us from pride that turns people
    away from You.
Save us from discouragement that
    causes us to lose hope.
Resource our marriage so it is a
    sanctuary of tender affection.

And make our ministry effective for the
strengthening
of Your people and the fulfillment of
our call. Amen

H. B. London, Jr. and Neil Wiseman, Married to
a Pastor's Wife

Open up before GOD, keep nothing
back;
 he'll do whatever needs to be done:
He'll validate your life in the clear light
of day
 and stamp you with approval at high
noon.

Psalm 37:5-6, THE MESSAGE

"For I know the plans that I have for
you," declares the LORD, "plans for wel-
fare and not for calamity to give you a
future and a hope."

Jeremiah 29:11, NASB

In conclusion be strong—not in yourselves but in the Lord, in the power of his
boundless strength.

Ephesians 6:10, PHILLIPS

Remember your call!
If we lose the sense of wonder of our
commission, we shall become like com-

mon traders in a common market, babbling about common wares.

John Jowett, The Preacher: His Life and Work

If the pastor can once again acknowledge that surely he was called, he is ready to find encouragement in his own answers to the following questions:

1. Who is the One who called me?
2. Who is the One I am serving?
3. Who is the One I must please?
4. Who is the One who empowers me for service?
5. Who is the One who will reward me for faithfulness?

For a pastor, the answers to these questions can bring relief to deep anguish, shed light in the darkness of despair, offer healing to the open raw wounds of spiritual conflict, correct deflated egos, provide renewing power for service, and give motivation, enthusiasm and joy in faithful service until the race is completed. This is genuine encouragement from God Himself.

Willard L. Davis

ACKNOWLEDGMENTS

Grateful acknowledgment is made to the publishers of the following Scripture versions:

Scripture quotations marked AMP are from *The Amplified Bible,* © 1954, 1958, 1987 by The Lockman Foundation. Used by permission.

Scripture quotations marked CEV are from the *Contemporary English Version* © 1995 by Thomas Nelson Inc.

Scripture quotations marked GOD'S WORD are from GOD'S WORD, a copyrighted work of God's Word to the Nations Bible Society. All rights reserved.

Scripture quotations marked KJV are from *The Holy Bible, 21st Century King James Version* (KJ21®), ©1994, Deuel Enterprises, Inc., Gary, SD, and used by permission.

Scripture quotations marked THE MESSAGE are from *The Message,* © 1993, 1994, 1995 by Eugene H. Peterson. Used by permission of NavPress Publishing Group.

Scripture quotations marked NASB are from the New American Standard Bible, © 1960, 1962, 1963, 1968, 1971, 1972, 1973, 1975, 1977 by The Lockman Foundation. Used by permission.

Scripture quotations marked NIV are from the HOLY BIBLE, NEW INTERNATIONAL VERSION ®. NIV ®. © 1973, 1978, 1984 by International Bible Society. Used by permission of Zondervan Publishing House. All rights reserved. The "NIV" and "New International Version" trademarks are registered in the United States Patent and Trademark Office by International Bible Society. Use of either trademark requires permission of the International Bible Society.

Scripture quotations marked NKJV are from *The New King James Version.* © 1979, 1980, 1982, Thomas Nelson Inc., Publishers.

Scripture quotations marked NLT are from the *Holy Bible,* New Living Translation, © 1996. Used by permission of Tyndale House Publishers, Inc., Wheaton, Illinois 60189. All rights reserved.